To D.
Wishir
Best
Jeffrey.

POSITIVE
THOUGHTS
FOR TODAY

You are great Leader friend
and partner!

Always
the
Best

Jeffrey Abdool

Cover Design by Elena Makansi
Cover Photo by Elena Makansi

ISBN: 978-0-692-48183-7

To My beloved wife Martha: You are my best friend and each day I am humbled and appreciative of your loving heart, faith, and support.

To Pearl and Jeff: Mom/Dad – Thanks for your wholehearted love for the Lord and the faithful example you have provided to our family.

To Joanna, Laura, Melissa, friends at my firm, and business mentors: Thanks for encouraging me each day and for inspiring me to become the Leader you expected me to be!

POSITIVE THOUGHTS FOR TODAY

Today and always, do not allow yourselves to drift away from having a great thought-life. Remember, master your mind, discipline your thoughts, and stay confident that your mission, vision, and goals will come to pass!

DAY 1

Today, ratchet up your passion! Remember, there is no substitute for passion. It is fuel for the will, and it will help you achieve your goals - especially when you want something badly enough. Remember, when you have a strong desire to achieve Success, you find the willpower to achieve it. So today, ratchet up your passion, and increase your intensity as you strive for Excellence!

DAY 2

PASSION

Today, do your very best in all that you do, and you will experience lasting Success! Remember, truly successful people have learned to do the things that do not naturally come together. So today, remember that sometimes real Success resides in experiencing aversion and achieving breakthroughs in spite of it.

So always love your Life. Remember, each day is a gift and a means to Celebrate. So today, enjoy each moment, throw your heart into all that you do, willingly share your wisdom, expect the best in all things and let your passion draw out the passion of others!

DAY 3

Today, refocus your thinking, rethink your approach, and repeat the process. Remember, see the solution in every challenge, be solution-oriented, think through what may be a seemingly impossible issue, redefine the situation, and if at first you do not succeed, keep at it. Always see the solution within every challenge!

DAY 4

TRANSFORMATION

Today, let your positive attitude transform every challenge into an opportunity! Remember, every challenge has an opportunity, and every opportunity has a challenge.

So today, allow yourself to dwell in the positive moments, cultivating a positive attitude, and regularly feeding your mind materials that will encourage you to have and maintain a positive outlook!

DAY 5

Today, start with your end goal in view. To do this, you will have to muster up energy and direction. To attain this, you will need to let your passion pull you forward. So let your planning set your direction. Remember that you cannot win if you do not begin. So today, begin your task with positive thinking, and always anticipate finishing strong, finishing well, and underscoring all of what you do with Excellence!

DAY 6

POSITIVE IMPACT

Today, focus on things you can do something about, and do not let what you cannot do interfere with what you can do! Remember, as you move forward on your Success journey, you need to understand that what happens *in* you is more important than what happens *to* you. So today, remember that you have no control over the actions of others, but you can control your attitude, and this can have a more positive impact than you would ever imagine!

DAY 7

Today, give each situation a little more patience, a little more effort, and most of all, a little more persistence! Remember, when the clouds of discouragement come and attempt to obscure your sense of victory, your persistence will always pay off and allow you to see the unseen! So today, turn each challenging situation into glorious Success and victory!

DAY 8

TAKE ACTION

Today, look for opportunities to help and support those who are in need. Thereafter, do your very best to fill those needs by going a step beyond the expectations of the people you serve. Remember, it's no accident that you are striving to operate at the highest standards of Excellence! So today, let your actions be a direct result of how you feel and see yourself.

DAY 9

Today, choose to take the high road, and conduct yourself according to the highest standards of Excellence! Remember, people who take the high road and make Excellence their goal will often care more, risk more, dream more, work more, and expect more than others may think is possible.

DAY 10

NO LIMITS

Today, embrace opportunities that push the envelope, and take some chances to explore new solutions as you drive toward Excellence. Remember, one of the secrets of Success is not letting what you cannot do interfere with what you can do! So today, keep going, be persistent, try something a little harder, and push those boundaries to their limits!

DAY 11

Today is a new day, so take time to renew your commitment, and reflect upon the benefits that come from doing this every day! Remember, always focus on your choices, rather than the situation!

JEFFREY ABDOOL

DAY 12

ACT WITH INTEGRITY

Today, when serving others, listen carefully, listen attentively, listen aggressively, and, most of all, listen with your whole heart! Remember, when your hearts are on high receive, you are acting with Integrity. And when you are listening this way, it creates a sustainable capacity for you and others to achieve greater purpose!

DAY 13

Today, think about an impossible issue or situation you have been challenged to overcome. Now, make up your mind to be determined that you will not give up until you find a solution! Remember, no matter what the situation might be, staying solution-oriented will cause you to find the power to overcome!

DAY 14

BECOME A CATALYST

Today, let each challenge become a catalyst that drives you forward and closer to attaining and achieving Success. Remember, we all, at one point or another, come to a place where capacity and capability are stretched beyond our abilities and gifts, but when you take time to reflect on yesterday's victories and leverage this strength, it will help you build your confidence. Remember that when you realize that the same Success that was attained yesterday can be accomplished again today, every challenge will become a catalyst that drives you forward!

DAY 15

Today, take time to examine each past Success or failure and understand that each experience is a source of Wisdom and information. Remember, every learning moment can teach you more about your particular gifts and talents. So today, leverage your gifts, and put them into motion so that each person you encounter gets infected by nothing less than Excellence!

DAY 16

SUCCESS

Today, the measure of your Success is not whether you have a tough issue to deal with, but whether it is a repetitious issue. Remember, each issue solved becomes a springboard for future Success. So today, focus on what you are learning, and keep an open door to blending possibility, positive action, and your enthusiasm together. Do this well, and it will make a difference in all that you do!

DAY 17

Today, remember that adversity is the first path to truth. It is difficult to give general guidelines on how to learn from adversity because every situation is different. But if you maintain a teachable attitude as you approach a process and try to learn anything you can about what you could do differently, you will improve the situation and yourself. Remember, when a person has the right attitude and mindset, every obstacle becomes an opportunity to improve!

DAY 18

SOLUTION-ORIENTED

Today, set aside dedicated time with subject matter experts to work through issues; make sure that it's prime think time, and not leftover time where you can get distracted. Remember, no issue can withstand the assault of sustained thinking. So today, see the solution in every challenge and cultivate a solution-oriented attitude, and you will achieve Success!

DAY 19

Today, accept challenges as the price of Success and keep striving to move forward! Remember, the ingenious will always find ways to improve the productivity and profits of their organization, and along the way, they will also discover awesome opportunities to perform any type of work that will make new things happen! So today, if you are looking to achieve the highest levels of Excellence, remember that you must be willing to serve at lower levels, at the higher levels, and virtually at every level to reach the highest level!

DAY 20

PURPOSE-DRIVEN

Today, be purpose–driven, and use the following steps to develop that desire:

1. Collaborate with people who possess great desire.
2. Develop a discontent with the status quo.
3. Let your goals excite you!

Remember, let your attitude determine how far you will go in your Success journey!

DAY 21

Today, think outside of the box, and push processes toward those limits that will help you achieve Success! Remember, when you encounter folks that want to make improvements, retire old rules, invent new procedures, and push boundaries to their limits, allow their commitment to be a catalyst that helps everyone you know meet their highest potential. Remember, each day you persist in improving, you are becoming a little bit better than you were the previous day!

DAY 22

BE INTENTIONAL

Today, work with a higher sense of purpose, focus on the right things, moment to moment, day to day, and then follow through in a consistent way! Remember, always be intentional and make every action count!

DAY 23

Today, allow your positive attitude to help determine how you see and handle each challenge or situation. Remember, when you change your lens and allow your attitude to be your greatest asset, it will help you drive forward and up the mountain of Success!

JEFFREY ABDOOL

DAY 24

QUALITY AND HEART

Today, let your character enable you to do what is right even when things seem challenging! Always remember that the quality of your actions spring from the quality of your heart!

Remember, always think big and start small! So today, if you are going to win you will need to begin by leveraging each incremental accomplishment and letting that provide you with energy, motivation and encouragement toward accomplishing the next steps out in front of you. Remember, small beginnings afford you the opportunity to prioritize, concentrate, and Succeed!

DAY 25

Today, be generous with your time and energy. Remember that giving is the highest level of living! So today, make a positive impact by giving to others!

Embrace your ability to influence others and always choose Excellence in everything you do. Remember, Excellence is choice. So today, pay close attention to the details, seek continual improvement, be disciplined, and stay committed. Remember, you have the power to decide how far you can go on your Success journey ... so always strive for Excellence and keep reaching to attain your highest potential!

DAY 26

ENDURANCE

Today, endure, improve, and overcome! Remember that in trying times, you should not quit trying. Rather, you should search deep down inside, and allow your heart to help you press forward with determination well beyond what you think you can achieve!

DAY 27

Today and always, be confident that you can accomplish anything that you need to do. Remember, the greatest achievers remain confident regardless of circumstance. So today, have confidence, and allow this to be one of the characteristics that propel you toward reaching your goals.

DAY 28

CONVICTION AND ACTION

Today, believe in what you say, then live what you say. Remember, there is no greater credibility than putting your convictions into action! So today, always remember that the goal of everything that you put your mind to must be actionable!

DAY 29

Today, start the day thinking about how you will move forward and cultivate an attitude that will give you the best opportunity for Success! Remember, when you are intentional about learning something new every day, you become better prepared to handle whatever challenges may lie ahead.

DAY 30

CONFIDENCE

Today, be confident and competent with the details; distill what is best and execute with Excellence. Remember, when you believe in something, the victory is won because you have discovered what you need in order to keep you going!

So focus on the big picture and remember, you have a purpose and it is entirely important that you plan, execute, and make the decision to do your very best at finishing everything that you start. Today, develop a habit of changing any excuses into reasons to pursue Excellence ... soon you will see that those positives trade offs ... are taking you further on your Success journey!

DAY 31

Today and always, never settle for average results, pay close attention to the details, perform with consistency, and stay committed to Excellence! Remember, Excellence will gauge your value by measuring you against your own potential.

DAY 32

POSITIVE DEFINING MOMENTS

Positive defining moments can help define who you are! Today, no matter how tough it gets or what kind of storm comes, use each moment as an opportunity to learn, grow, improve, serve, and distinguish yourself as a possibility thinker! Remember, if you believe you can, you can and you will. So today, be intentional about everything that you do. Learn from each challenge, and maintain a mindset where you live and learn. Continually do this, and you will really learn how to live!

DAY 33

Today, know your strengths as well as your areas of opportunity! Remember, leveraging your strengths allows you to rekindle your passion and renew your energy! So today, take positive action, and be intentional about leveraging your strengths and keeping your priorities on target!

DAY 34

POSITIVE BENEFITS

Today, embrace adversity, and retrain yourself to view each challenging experience as a way to move forward! Remember, when you step back from an unexpected circumstance and view each experience through a forward-looking lens, you will discover the positive benefits of adversity!

DAY 35

Today, if conditions get difficult, step up your tenacity, and work with a higher sense of expectation and determination. Remember that in trying times you should not quit trying. So today, push beyond what you think you can do, and you will find out that you really are capable of accomplishing so much more Success than you ever thought!

DAY 36

SELF-DISCIPLINE

Today, operate with self-discipline and inner trust, and make a decision to relentlessly be honest in all situations of your life. Remember, let your Integrity be the glue that holds your way of life together, and constantly strive to protect and keep your Integrity intact!

DAY 37

Today, embrace Wisdom and your ability to see life with objectivity! Remember, Wisdom gives you balance, strength, and the insight to handle all challenges with grace and stability!

DAY 38

TRIUMPHANT

Today, remember that embracing Wisdom at work and in your life affords you the ability to act, respond, and execute with calm confidence and Service Excellence!

So today view failures as lesson-learned moments and remember that failing forward is a critical part of Success. So leverage the success of those moments where the end result may not have been quite what you may have hoped. Remember that every Successful attempt forward eventually leads to being triumphant.

DAY 39

Today, surround yourself with good thinkers, and be highly intentional about the thinking process. Remember, put yourself in the right place to think, shape, stretch, and land your ideas. Make this a priority, and always remember that good thinking takes discipline!

DAY 40

PRESS FORWARD

Today, embrace the desire to achieve Success, and master the process of being highly intentional in everything that you do! Remember, to elevate your standard of living, you will need to be thinking and embracing the highest-level thinking!

So today, should you encounter a challenging situation that may be seemingly difficult, remember that you are very capable of rising above the common plain and achieving Success. Stay determined, have faith, embrace hope, and do not quit. Success is always achieved by those who keep on trying and pressing forward!

DAY 41

Today, raise your expectations, and seek to go higher than the standards that may be set before you! Remember, great people are not ever satisfied with their current level of performance! They are demanding of themselves and always push hard to reach their highest potential!

DAY 42

EMPOWERMENT

Today, enjoy the freedom of empowerment and of making good choices! Remember that when you make a decision, you become a servant to that choice! And you must deal with its consequence whether it is for better or for worse. So today, remember that successful people will make the right decisions early and manage those decisions every day!

DAY 43

Today, be grateful for whatever you have, and courageously do the things you are most afraid to do. Remember that every time you stand up under the weight of adversity you are being prepared for something great!

So today, should you encounter a challenging situation that may be seemingly difficult, remember that you are very capable of rising above the common plain and achieving Success. So stay faithful, hopeful, and do not quit. Success is always achieved by those who keep on persisting and pressing forward!

DAY 44

DILIGENCE

Today, remain diligent in doing well and encourage others to do likewise. Remember that your actions always reflect who you are on the inside as well as how disciplined you are!

DAY 45

Today, keenly focus on your current responsibilities so that you can have a better tomorrow! Remember that your Success journey starts from right where you are, not from where you think you should be!

So remember, the greatest thing you need to achieve Success resides in your abilities to connect, appreciate, trust and be in harmony with all those that you interact with. So today, dedicate yourselves toward thinking it forward and having an attitude where you are increasingly giving, serving, and investing in the Success of others. Remember the highest level of living will always come from giving!

JEFFREY ABDOOL

DAY 46

REMAIN TEACHABLE

Today, remain teachable - try something new, and go out of your way to do something different that will stretch you professionally, mentally, emotionally, or physically. Remember, if what you did yesterday still looks big to you, you have not accomplished much! So meet each challenge head on, and allow each experience to help change you for the better!

DAY 47

Remember, to succeed you must act with absolute Integrity! So today, add the power of purpose to this characteristic, and you will keep your emotional fire and desire for Success burning long and strong!

DAY 48

EXCELLENCE

Today and always, follow through with Excellence! Remember, when you are following through, you are often performing at the highest level of Excellence. This is always a choice and act of will!

DAY 49

Today and always, choose to model good character! Remember, your character determines your view on life, and how you see the world around you has a direct impact on each action you take. So today, let your character exemplify traits of goodness, kindness, gentleness, generosity, and selflessness!

DAY 50

PREPARATION

Today, remember that courage has no greater ally than preparation and remember that fear has no greater enemy! So today, commit yourself to doing the right things right, following through on your purpose, aligning your values and striking a balance to maintain a healthy pace - that allows you to accomplish your goals and support your longer range goals.

DAY 51

Today, embrace possibility type thinking!
Remember that possibility thinkers are
capable of accomplishing tasks that seem
impossible because they believe in the
solutions they seek, drive, and deliver. So
today, open yourself up to possibility type
thinking, and you will soon open yourself up
to many more possibilities!

DAY 52

SUCCESS

Today, maintain good thinking, manage your energy, do all you can to serve others, and always be kind to others. Do this well and you will know Success! Remember, all good things will work together when you are seeking to achieve results that are for a higher purpose!

DAY 53

Today, use the clarity of mountaintop moments to make major decisions! Remember, if you keep on persevering and make it to higher ground, you will develop the type of character that will serve you well throughout your entire life!

DAY 54

CONFIDENCE

Today, no matter what issue or circumstance you encounter, remember that responding in a positive manner will produce the best results!

So today, have great confidence over everything you say, do, and deliver. Remember, your beliefs determine how you live and impact the outcome of everything you do. So make it your goal to compound your daily practice with a high level of confidence. Remember, everything you are doing today is preparing you for a better and greater tomorrow.

DAY 55

Today, remember that there is no move in life that is more eloquent and effective than one that is continually and consistently based on Integrity!

Remember your thinking ability is influenced by present and past experiences. So to become a great thinker, you will need to become a good thinker first ... once this happens, ideas will start flowing, things will positively improve, and each day will get better and better. So today, maintain your passion, become a great thinker and leverage your integrity!

DAY 56

PERSPECTIVE

Today, harness the power of new and fresh perspectives. Remember, one of the best ways to innovate, create, and flex your solutions is to be on the lookout for fresh ideas and to keenly listen to the observations of others. So today, take time to reflect on yesterday and honestly evaluate its Successes and challenges. This will help you prepare for tomorrow! Remember, your willingness to learn and adjust positively will help you continually move forward on your Success journey!

DAY 57

Today, rise above the common plain and apply a little more determination to meet and exceed your goals! Remember that great and successful people are simply ordinary people that have tapped into an extraordinary amount of determination to be successful in all that they do! Today, be one of those people!

DAY 58

COMMITMENT

Today, embrace possibility type thinking! Remember that when you remove the label of "impossible" from any task, you raise your potential from average to off the charts!

So today do what is right and let your character bring you lasting Success. Remember, as you work through your daily agenda, recognize that your character and commitment elevates you and will cause you to persevere. So, embrace Excellence, raise your thinking to new levels, and strive to keep your daily commitments in a way that you are working hard for what you believe in and striving to accomplish something you once believed was impossible!

DAY 59

Today, focus your thoughts so they are filled with Integrity, Vision, Vitality, and Victory. Remember that positive thinking will help you grow stronger and give you the momentum needed to achieve Success!

DAY 60

POSITIVE ACTION

Today, see it like it could be! Remember that when something has seized you and caused you to have a high level of commitment, those are the greatest days of your lives! So today, let's go for it! Get your hearts and minds around the concept of focused thinking and listening. Remember, when you listen with emotional intelligence – it results in action, interaction, and demonstrates that you value the people you are communicating with. So today – see it like it could be and remember that one of the greatest gifts you can give a client, partner, colleague, or family member is the gift of paying close attention to what their hearts are saying.

DAY 61

Today, no matter how you feel, take it a step further, keep on improving, follow through with Excellence, and always accomplish more than is expected! Remember that highly competent people will always take responsibility to its highest level!

DAY 62

SUCCESS

Today, do your job with laser-like focus! Remember, accomplish your top priorities first, work purposefully and strategically, and focus on what is important rather than what is easy. Do this consistently, and you will experience Success!

DAY 63

Today, be an encourager, and take a servant's mindset as you bring a positive outcome to everything that you do. So today, embrace this mindset and you can soar to the highest level of Excellence! Remember that every interaction with a client, associate, or business partner is an opportunity to express kindness.

DAY 64

PASSION

Today, as you go through your day, remember to be a good listener. Listen attentively, listen humbly, and listen with your heart. Soon you will begin to learn things that will help you to expand your knowledge, talent, and ability to deliver and drive Excellence. Remember, every challenge is an opportunity to learn, grow, and serve!

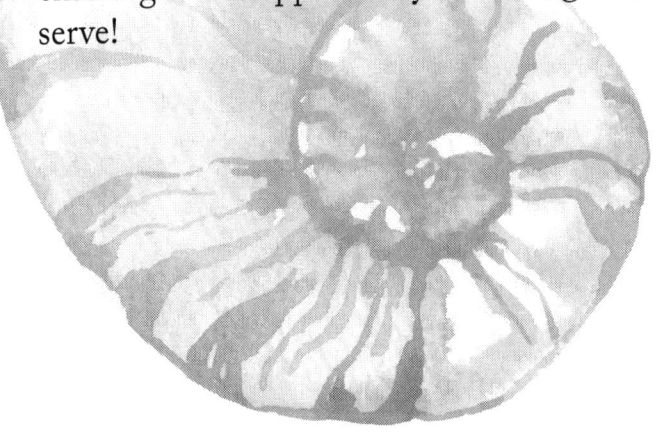

DAY 65

Today and always, be compassionate, caring, and selfless as you serve one another. Remember that Success can bring many things: power, privilege, fame, wealth, etc. But no matter what it brings, with Success you will always have options. So today, leverage those options to reveal a character that emanates goodness to all those that you serve.

DAY 66

ACCOMPLISHMENTS

Today, try your hardest, do your very best, choose a direction, and focus your attention and efforts so that you can completely provide the highest and best level of service to your clients! Remember that each time you achieve one thing, you are creating stepping stones that will help you go higher up the mountain of accomplishments!

DAY 67

Today, concentrate on continually improving! Remember, sharpen your mind, control your emotions, and focus your actions so that each day you become a little better than you were yesterday!

Seek out all opportunities. Remember, the best way to find an opportunity is to pursue the one at hand. So today, be an opportunist and make the most of each moment, evaluate all options and continually look for ways to achieve and reach your highest potential.

DAY 68

SUCCESS

Remember that Teamwork, Excellence, Faith, Discipline, Dedication, Focus, and Leadership are some of the tools that characterize and embody Success! So today, as you focus on your Mission, Vision, and Values, leverage these characteristics, and be the best you can be in each endeavor you undertake!

DAY 69

Today, leverage pivotal moments to bring about positive change and lasting breakthrough moments! Remember that breakthrough moments happen when you seize the opportunity presented by a significant event!

DAY 70

EXPECTANCY

Today, work with joy and expectancy! Remember that when you work with your whole heart and a sustained perspective of Excellence, your desire to attain Success will come to fruition!

DAY 71

Today, mellow your hearts and humble your spirits. Remember, when you are more sensitive to proper values and empathetic toward the less fortunate, you will discover the truth about Success.

DAY 72

INTEGRITY

Today, be too large to worry, too noble for anger, too strong for fear, and too happy to permit any issue to pressure you! Remember, let your character and Integrity precede everything that you do!

DAY 73

Today, prepare, plan, practice, and execute with the belief that you will succeed in everything that you do! Remember that if you are faced with adversity, do not flinch, do not worry, and do not lose hope! Remember, a positive perspective is important, so believe, call it forward, and have faith knowing that you will overcome!

DAY 74

SERVICE EXCELLENCE

Today, work with great intensity! Grind it out, work through the emotions, realize your competency level, and bring out your full potential to drive Service Excellence to all of those that you serve! Remember, your attitude at the beginning of any task will affect its outcome more than anything else!

DAY 75

Today, focus on the upside! Remember, maintain a positive perspective, do your very best, and always work with joy, peace, patience, goodness, self-control, high expectancy and kindness!

DAY 76

QUALITY

Today, cultivate the qualities of politeness and good manners as you drive Service Excellence to all those that you serve! Remember that if you want to experience Excellence, you have to be willing to give, deliver, and provide Excellence in everything that you do!

DAY 77

Today, work with quiet confidence, embrace Excellence, and allow your winning attitude to be a key driver in everything that you do! Remember that a good attitude always permeates through a successful person and organization.

DAY 78

EXCELLENCE

Today, be a strong finisher, prepare for everything you do, ready yourself to bring your task to completion, and concentrate on finishing with Excellence. Remember that along your Success journey you may encounter some challenging situations, but those of you who are committed to finishing strong will always get back on track, press on, and follow through until your work is complete! So today, finish well and finish strong!

DAY 79

Today, push yourself beyond your comfort zones, and challenge yourself to wrestle with the biggest obstacles in your pathway. Remember, there is a choice in everything that you do, and the choice that you make can positively make you!

DAY 80

SUCCESS

Remember that when you do your very best, you have achieved Success! So today, embrace this simple truth and you will experience tremendous strength and satisfaction!

Remember, the best way to find an opportunity is to pursue the one at hand. So today, be an opportunist and make the most of each moment, evaluate all options, and continually look for ways to achieve and reach your highest potential!

DAY 81

Today, keep your standards high. In every situation, give everything that you have, and always walk with your head held up high! Remember that the result will take care of itself when you take care of the effort that precedes the result!

So today and always stay true to your principles, beliefs and gifts.Remember,when you stay true your values, you increase your potential for sustainable Success. So stay committed to your goals, keep on developing an attitude of Excellence, share your knowledge, work with a high sense of urgency and allow your character to enable you to rise above any limitation!

DAY 82

BE INTENTIONAL

When you think about your Success journey, remember that Success is continual and it is an ongoing process, but most of all, it is the positive result of steady and forward movement! So today, be intentional about everything that you do, and work with the purpose of making every action count! Focus on doing the right things in the right way, and then follow through in a consistent manner!

DAY 83

Today, do everything you can to serve your community well. Concentrate on this goal, and focus your potential on continually exceeding people's expectations. Remember that the true measure of Success is the ratio between what may happen and what you will become. In other words, Success comes as a result of growing to your highest potential and soaring to heights that go well beyond your imagination!

DAY 84

INTEGRITY

Today, set completion dates for your projects and tasks. Look for efficient ways to get the job done, and always take the time to share improvements and ideas. Remember, it matters how hard you work, but it matters more how smart you work! So today and always stay true to your principles, beliefs, and gifts. Remember, when you stay true to your values, you increase your potential for sustainable Success. So stay committed to your goals, keep on developing an attitude of Excellence, share your knowledge, work with a high sense of urgency and allow your character to enable you to rise above any limitation!

DAY 85

Today, as you set out to achieve results and deliver solutions, always act with the utmost Integrity and in a manner that shows personal regard for the people you serve. Remember that you can engineer a solution and resolve issues in a manner that will shape your future. So today, embrace this strategy as you serve your community and drive forward on solutions that emanate Service Excellence!

DAY 86

CHARACTER

Today, let your character enable you to do what is right even when things seem challenging! Remember that the quality of your actions spring from the quality of your heart!

So today remember, that our first defense against a negative situation will change when we: define the issue, gather information from credible resources, brainstorm on options, seek advice from the right people, listen to our instincts, and make decisions based on the principles/values we believe in. So today, be Successful in all that you do, and make sure you are following your heart.

DAY 87

Today and always, do your very best to exceed
expectations in everything you do. Remember,
to be successful, you need to set the bar
high for yourself, perform with Excellence,
and make it your goal to learn, grow, have a
limitless mindset, and exceed expectations
every time you have the opportunity to serve!

DAY 88

SUCCESS

Today, start moving forward, build up your momentum, and whatever you do, keep on going! Remember that a life spent moving from failure to mistakes to Success is more honorable than doing nothing at all!

So today and always, collaborate on ways to accomplish your goals. Remember, the best way to approach a tough challenge is to try to see each situation as an opportunity. So be a catalyst for turnaround, help everyone you can solve problems and always work to make things better!

DAY 89

Today, take time to determine the first step you need to take to achieve your main objective. Remember, examine each issue, size up the situation, and then get yourself motivated to spring into action!

DAY 90

EXCELLENCE

Today, when the adverse winds of challenging
situations occur, allow them
to be a force that will lift you higher!
Remember, your attitude toward life
determines life's attitude toward you.

So let today be the day you strive for
Excellence, expect the best, and rise above
each challenge!

DAY 91

Today, remember that Success is a state of mind. So today, if you want to achieve Success, you have to have courage, strength, and resilience! Always remember that no matter how difficult or challenging a circumstance may be, you can always find a way to persevere. This is the culture you need to promote and always embrace.

DAY 92

PASSION

Today, remember that your passion will dictate your first step toward any great achievement! So today, ratchet up your fire, and allow this energy to be a catalyst that will fuel your desire and provide you with energy and high potential to achieve Success!

DAY 93

Today, know your strengths as well as your areas of opportunity! Remember, leveraging your strengths allows you to rekindle your passion and renew your energy! So today, take positive action and be intentional about keeping your mind focused, your energy maximized, and your priorities on target!

DAY 94

DETERMINATION

Today, push beyond what you think you can do, and you will find out that you are really capable of accomplishing more than you would ever imagine. Remember, when conditions get difficult, it is time to step up your tenacity and work with higher expectation and determination. So today, if you are faced with trying times, do not quit trying. Push forward, and you will see a difference every step of the way!

DAY 95

Today, put others first. Remember, every day make a conscious effort to deposit goodwill into your relationships with others. This means giving more than you expect to receive, loving others unconditionally, looking for ways to add value to others, and bringing joy to all those relationships you hold dear!

DAY 96

VICTORY

Today, commit yourself to long term victory and achievement! Remember, successful people always have a clear view and strong future orientation!

So today let every challenge bring out your greatest ambitions and abilities to be action-oriented. Remember, every situation allows you the opportunity to exercise Positive thinking. So, become free of worrying and practice the habit of faith, hope, and perseverance, and experience the strength that comes from quieting yourself so that all these insights come through everything that you do.

DAY 97

Today, stick to your predetermined schedules and guard your time. This will put you in control of your agenda and allow you to function at your best! Remember that the key to scheduling is telling your time where to go instead of wondering where it went. So today, take command of your time and schedule.

DAY 98

POSITIVE FOCUS

Today, be delightful and generous, and instinctively fix your minds on whatever is good and positive! Remember that in this life, the measure of a person isn't the number of people who serve you; it is a matter of how many that you serve! So today, as you climb the mountain of Success, increase your level of giving and you will soar like an eagle to the highest levels of living!

DAY 99

Today - Learn (think big picture), Earn (keep your priorities on track), and Return (be generous with what you have, work hard, and plan well). Remember, each day practice patience, lay a good foundation for yourself, keep learning, keep growing, and do not ever give up!

DAY 100

INTEGRITY

Today, remember that Image is what people think you are, but Integrity is what you really are! So today, always act with Integrity because Integrity will not ever disappoint!

So today, remember, that no matter what has happened in the past, it's not ever too late to rise above your past experiences, have a bigger purpose and go higher than the common plain. So do not compromise, embrace and envision a brighter beginning, do what is right and always work with motives that exude Excellence!

DAY 101

Today, go into your day expecting the best. Remember that a good attitude makes it possible for you to be successful, and it will give you fuel so that you can pursue your purpose, grow to your potential, and plant seeds that will benefit others.

DAY 102

POSITIVE ATTITUDE

Today, soften your attitude, learn humility, and always remain teachable. Remember, no matter how much we know (or think we know), we can learn from every situation. With this type of thinking, you can turn every adversity into an advantage!

So today be intentional about equipping others to Succeed. Remember the one thing you can do to create the greatest impact on another person is to be intentional everyday about equipping others with the knowledge you gain, the lessons you learn, the principles you apply, and the steps you take to move forward on your Success journey. Do this well and you will reach your highest potential!

DAY 103

Today, if you want your talent to be lifted to its highest level, then don't begin by focusing just on your talent. Begin by harnessing the power of your mind. Remember that your beliefs control everything that you do. So today, believe positively and expect to succeed, and sure enough you will!

DAY 104

POSITIVE ATTITUDE

Today, remember that the quality of your life and duration of your Success depend on your attitude! Remember, the mind and your beliefs, more than anything else, determine how far you can go on your Success journey. So today, act your way into feeling positive, and when you face adversity, leverage this experience as an opportunity that will help you increase all your possibilities for achieving Success!

DAY 105

Today, work with vision, joy, high levels of expectancy, and with all of your heart! Remember, sustained Excellence is not accomplished by those who are half-hearted.

So today be an encourager and let your encouragement fuel your soul, so that whatever you share will fuel the recipient with power to overcome and achieve great things. Remember, be liberal with encouraging each other and soon you will see that everyone/everything is getting better and better!

DAY 106

CONFIDENCE

Today is going to be a great day! Remember, be bold, be confident, throw your hearts into all that you do, and remember that truly successful people have learned to do what does not come naturally and despite any aversion, they achieve breakthrough moments. So today, let all that you do be fully consumed with Excellence!

DAY 107

Today, fire up your furnace, go into your day with a greater sense of urgency and a higher sense of enthusiasm, and always be willing to go the extra mile for everyone you serve! Strive for Excellence and always expect the very best of everything. Remember, your attitude toward life determines life's attitude toward you!

DAY 108

DETERMINATION

Today, as you move forward on your Success journey, remember that the things that are happening in you are more important than the things that are happening outside of you. Remember that an Act of will leads you to action! And positive Action will lead you to a positive attitude!

So today embrace the opportunity to help one another and use your skills, gifts and talents to drive everything you touch to a higher purpose. Remember, that when we serve with a selfless attitude and focus on helping others achieve their goals everyone Wins and Succeeds!

DAY 109

Today, cultivate an inward determination to achieve your goals. Remember, when you have faced or experienced adversity, you are actually in a better position to achieve Success. So today, continually learn from these experiences, and you will build strength, tenacity, experience, and Wisdom. This is an essential part of sustained Success!

DAY 110

PASSION

Today, ratchet up your passion. Remember that anyone who lives beyond an ordinary life has great desire. So today, choose to overcome any challenge or obstacle, and leverage your passion, enthusiasm, and energy toward achieving Success!

Remember, be patient and Act with courage. Because, courage will allow you to be positive and overcome those things that are most challenging to you. So today, face each circumstance with courage, integrity, character, discipline, and the confidence of knowing that you are doing your very best to reach your highest potential!

DAY III

Today, start doing what is necessary, then start doing what is possible, and suddenly you will be doing what you thought was impossible. Remember, when you have an open mind, it is the beginning of self-discovery and growth. So today, focus your energy and always get things done with Excellence!

DAY 112

PREPARATION

Every day of our lives is a preparation for the next, and what we become tomorrow is a direct result of each action we take today. So today, groom yourselves for Success and remember that what we do today is preparing us for a bigger and brighter tomorrow.

DAY 113

Today, remember that passion is the first step toward achievement. As such, your desire determines your destiny. Remember, when a person has a weak desire, it will yield weak results. So today, have a great desire and raise your expectancy levels so you can achieve Success and deliver Excellence!

DAY 114

POSITIVE ATTITUDE

Today, cultivate a positive attitude, and regularly feed your mind motivational and positive materials that will encourage you to have and maintain a positive outlook! Remember, always allow yourself to dwell in the positive moments and not in the negative.

DAY 115

Today, remember that Integrity is not a given factor in everyone's life. It is a result of self-discipline, inner trust, and a decision to be relentlessly honest in all situations in our lives. Remember that Integrity is the glue that holds our way of life together. So today, you must constantly strive to keep your Integrity intact!

DAY 116

SUCCESS

Today, let your positive attitude transform every challenge into an opportunity. Remember, every challenge has an opportunity, and every opportunity has a challenge and a person's attitude determines how they handle each and whether they succeed and can move forward.

DAY 117

Today, concentrate on your highest priorities first and progress forward with Excellence in all that you do. Remember, to reach your highest potential, you will need to focus on the hardest things first, understand your purpose, and then act on doing the things you know need to get done!

DAY 118

INTEGRITY

Today and always, be honorable in all you do. Remember, make the right choices sooner, always act with Integrity, enable your inner and outer circles to visualize the positive aspects of what you are doing, and remember that Success is not for the chosen few, but for the few who have chosen to achieve Success!

DAY 119

Today, leverage your intuition. Remember, when you have great intuition, you have a head start on achieving your goals. So today, concentrate fast, take steps to size each condition, focus on current events, plan for each moment, and visualize a bright and successful future!

DAY 120

PURPOSE

Today, focus on the big picture. Remember, we all have a purpose, and it is entirely important that we plan, execute, and make the decision to do our very best at finishing everything that we start. So today, develop a habit of changing any excuses into reasons to pursue Excellence. Soon you will see that those positive trades offs are taking you further on your Success journey!

DAY 121

Today, be optimistic and confident in all that you do. Remember, affirm only the best for yourself and others, meet daily challenges gracefully, and always complete each daily task with confidence!

So today, leverage your experience and intuition for practical advice/solutions. Remember, the courage within you (your heart) will keep you committed and doing the right things regardless of the circumstance. So today, keep a good perspective, stay teachable, compromise on nothing, and fulfill on everything!

DAY 122

MOTIVATED

Today, get motivated and see what you can do to add value to others, expand your knowledge, and improve the quality of all that you do! Remember, if you do what you've always done, your result will always be the same. So today, always do and give more than is expected and soon you will see bigger and more promising results!

DAY 123

Today, sharpen your skills and seize all opportunities! Remember, focus on your actions, and deliver the type of quality services that differentiate you from the competition! This can be your unique advantage and should be your strategy for Success!

DAY 124

EXCELLENCE

Today, no matter how small the agreement you make with someone, do not forget about it or blow it off. Doing so creates a negative connotation and may inadvertently create a bad perception. Remember, trust is built through a series of consistent interactions in which agreements are made and kept. So today and every day, follow through on your word, follow through with Excellence and follow through in a manner that creates a lasting and Positive impact!

DAY 125

Today, embrace positive action, and use this power to go further on your Success journey. Remember, the quality of your life and the duration of your Success depend on your attitude, and you are the only person who can leverage this power to make today better!

So today get yourself into the right frame of mind before you start your day. Remember, everything you do colors your perspective. So today and always, be of sound character, communicate with credibility, be consistent, rise above any or every limitation, and allow your good characteristics to bring you lasting Success!

DAY 126

POSITIVE ACTION

Today, take time to appreciate and collaborate with each other, and let your partners and colleagues know how much you need them. Remember, no matter how successful you are, no matter how important or accomplished you are, we all need each other to succeed!

So embrace the power of collaboration and persistence. Keep your word, give your services away, always maintain a thankful heart and delight in the results that come from the passions that are raising you higher ... which is the power of Positive Action and Collaborative Persistence!

DAY 127

Today, if you feel like your fire is fizzling out, get around some igniters (i.e., people that can reignite you) because passion is contagious! Remember, Success breeds Success. So today, increase your passion and soar toward Success!

DAY 128

SUCCESS

Today, listen to others and remain humble, and you will begin to learn things that will help you resolve issues and succeed! Remember, a problem solved is a springboard for future Success. The key is to focus on what you are learning and to concentrate on what you are doing. So today, start from where you are – not from where you think you should be!

DAY 129

Today, release intimidation, doubt, and uncertainty, and renew your sense of purpose so you can develop, win, and succeed. Remember, the bigger the challenge, the more of an opportunity you have to succeed. So today, realize there are no challenges that you cannot conquer!

DAY 130

INTEGRITY

Today, remember that the importance of character increases as the business environment increases, especially during times of expansion and globalization. As such, people with good character are easily recognizable; they are always consistent no matter the circumstance. So today and always, let your Integrity shine through and be present in everything that you do!

DAY 131

Today, to achieve Success in any area, you always need to continually do things you have not done before, and sometimes that may mean you might falter. So remember, very successful people never lose energy and always keep forward progress at a fast pace!

DAY 132

SUCCESS

Today, when you serve your community, plant and sow seeds that will benefit others. Thereafter, you will reap all of the benefits of your Success. Remember that Success is knowing your purpose in life and it is an unwavering Act of growing, reaching, and achieving your highest potential!

DAY 133

Today, as you set completion dates for your projects and tasks, take time to look for efficient ways to get the job done, and share your findings when there is an opportunity for process improvement. Remember, it matters how hard you work, but it matters more how much smarter you make others work!

DAY 134

EXCELLENCE

Today, seek out your inner strength, and leverage that ability to deliver Service Excellence to all those that you serve. Remember, character makes trust possible. And trust makes Leadership possible, and the two together can make everything else possible!

So today get yourself into the right frame of mind before you start your day. Remember, everything you do colors your perspective. So always be of sound character, communicate with credibility, be consistent, rise above any or every limitation and allow your good characteristics to bring you lasting Success!

DAY 135

Today, as you set out to achieve results and deliver solutions, act with Integrity and in a manner that shows personal regard to the people you serve! Remember that this is the difference that can make the difference in everyone's lives!

DAY 136

POSITIVE ACTION

Today, continually invest your best efforts in each task, project, and solution. Soon you will find that your actions are compounding and resulting in significant growth! Remember that the secret of your Success is found in your daily agenda.

So today, leverage your experience and intuition for practical advice/solutions. Remember, the courage within you (your heart) will keep you committed and doing the right things regardless of circumstance. So today, keep a good perspective, stay teachable, compromise on nothing and fulfill on everything!

DAY 137

Today, be highly intentional! Look for opportunities to help people, be highly available, and ensure that each client, business partner, friend, or family member knows how important they are to your Success. Remember, the quality of your relationships depends on your depth and concern for others. This is the most important aspect in your ability to serve!

DAY 138

PURPOSE

Today, take joy in knowing your purpose, and raise your potential as you successfully deliver Excellence. Remember, you have a higher purpose and a unique responsibility to carry out each task or assignment for each person you are serving.

DAY 139

Today, take the opportunity to implement new techniques, and overwhelm your clients with Service Excellence. Your responsibility and greatest joy is achieving this each day. Remember, every person has a unique approach to fulfilling services to one another.

DAY 140

COMMITMENT

Today, do everything you can to serve your community well. Concentrate on this goal, and focus your potential on continually exceeding your clients' expectations. Soon you will reach your highest potential and experience Success beyond your imagination! Remember, Success comes through growth, dedication, and commitment!

DAY 141

Today, focus on improving yourself by expanding your knowledge and adding value to others. Remember, forget about your mistakes and focus on what you learned. Do this each day, and you will become better today as well as grow your potential for an even greater tomorrow!

DAY 142

SUCCESS

Today, remember that you are what you think you are. So make sure your thinking is on the right track, and always let your actions be the complete sum of your Success!

Remember, today and always it is crucial that you are genuine and authentic about everything you say and do. Remember, always communicate with honor, integrity, high value, and genuine commitment.

DAY 143

Today, embrace a high level of performance, and unleash your abilities to overcome every obstacle, challenge, and issue. Remember that it is easier to move from failure to Success than from excuses to Success. So today, release yourself from negative thinking, unleash your potential and spring into action!

DAY 144

EXCELLENCE

Today, embrace your ability to influence others and always choose Excellence in everything you do. Remember, Excellence is a choice. So today, pay close attention to the details, seek continual improvement, be disciplined, and stay committed. Remember, you have the power to decide how far you can go on your Success journey, so always strive for Excellence and keep reaching to attain your highest potential!

DAY 145

Today, seek out your most difficult tasks and challenges, and let your resilience and tenacity help you achieve Excellence! Always remember that successful people always take on the tough assignments and projects.

So today do not lose sight of the big picture. Remember, every situation has meaning, every interaction counts and everything we do has a bigger purpose. So today, maintain the desires of your hearts, fulfill the demands of each assignment and be purposeful in everything that you say and do!

DAY 146

EXPECT THE BEST

Today and always, think only the best, expect only the best, and let these motives drive you forward in your quest to deliver and experience Excellence!

So today and always, do not Act alone. Remember, when times get challenging, we all need to work together. So if a challenge escalates, then let teamwork elevate you. Remember, you cannot achieve Success unless you work together with others.

DAY 147

Today and always, believe in yourself, trust in your abilities, and have faith that everything you do or touch will surmount everyone's expectations (clients, partners, and family)!

DAY 148

SERVICE EXCELLENCE

Today, make sure that every person you interact with feels like the most important person in the world! Remember, to be successful in this area, you must be a good listener and serve with a loving heart.

DAY 149

Today, remember that time after time, Success comes down to sacrifice. The same is true for the teams that are always Successful. Each person must be willing to sacrifice time and energy to exceed client expectations. So today, let these motives cause you to attain uncommon results and solutions that continually cause you to achieve Excellence!

DAY 150

PERSISTENCE

Today, embrace strategies that continuously promote and help you deliver Service Excellence! Remember, you can architect solutions, design frameworks, innovate, and create Success through your hardworking persistence!

DAY 151

Today, unleash your enthusiasm and become emotionally involved in the solutions you are offering. Remember, your ability to communicate your knowledge is important, but your ability to share your belief is critically important! So today, get excited about everything you are doing!

DAY 152

INSPIRATION

Today and always, be grateful and inspired by great ideas, and gain a discontent with being in the same place for any extended period of time. Remember, be intentional and work with purpose. Commit yourself to a mission, a vision, and values that cause you to excel in everything you do!

DAY 153

Today, take the opportunity to implement new techniques, and overwhelm your clients with Service Excellence! Remember, everyone has a unique approach to fulfilling Service Excellence. So today, leverage your responsibility, and you will experience great joy as you set a course to meet your goals each day!

DAY 154

POSITIVE ATTITUDE

Today, having the right view of Success can help you keep a positive attitude about yourself, your life, and everything you do. Remember, always execute with Excellence, and remember that no matter what you've faced in your past, you have the potential to overcome all things!

DAY 155

Today, make every minute count and use your knowledge and power to bring forth Service Excellence! Always remember that successful people are doers that do not sit around idling.

DAY 156

OPPORTUNITY

Today, be a positive influencer! Remember, encourage each other daily, and take every opportunity to be kind to each person you come into contact with.... Remember, when you have an opportunity, every moment counts because every experience is filled with high potential. So today, do not take anything for granted; embrace every experience, push yourselves to Act, leverage your passion, see the potential in every situation, and always stay positive despite any circumstance!

DAY 157

Remember, highly competent people continually search for ways to learn, grow, and improve. So today and always, embrace a teachable strategy, and then sign everything that you do with Excellence!

DAY 158

EXCELLENCE

Today, perform at a high level of Excellence and remember that this is a choice and an act of will. Remember, highly competent people consistently perform at a high level and always go the extra mile!

DAY 159

Today and always, maintain a teachable attitude. Remember, to do this, you must remain humble, keep a learning attitude, and if you encounter an obstacle or make a mistake, always fail in a direction that allows you to continually progress forward!

DAY 160

COLLABORATE

Always remember that successful people admit faults, move from failure to Success, and do not ever make excuses. So today, learn from each moment, collaborate with others, overcome all obstacles, and always do more than expected!

DAY 161

Today, remember that having the right view of Success will help keep you positive about yourself, your friends, family, clients, and all circumstances. Remember, always do your very best every day!

DAY 162

SELFLESSNESS

Today, cultivate a service-mindset type of attitude with your clients, your colleagues, and everyone you interact with. Remember, at the heart of selflessness is generosity, and this type of loyalty fosters unity, and unity breeds a level of Success that impacts all those around you!

DAY 163

Today, remember that nothing improves a person's outlook like delivering services to someone with a greater need than their own!

DAY 164

OVERCOME

Today, embrace adversity and enhance your skills through each experience you encounter. Remember, the greatest achievement occurs through conquering repeated challenges!

DAY 165

Today, be grateful for the talents, skills, and gifts you have been blessed with. Remember, there may be many times that you may feel that there is something that you cannot accomplish. During these times, let your limitless attitude reflect the true essence of your Success. So today, remember that in life it's not what you have that makes a difference. It's how many people you help with what you have!

DAY 166

CHANGE

Who you are today is the result of the choices you made yesterday. Remember, tomorrow you can become what you choose today. So today, let change mean to choose the right type of change!

DAY 167

Today, remember that in order to overcome a challenging or difficult situation, you will have to have a great deal of faith. Remember, from the beginning to completion of each situation you will need to believe positively. With this mindset, you will be destined to achieve Success!

DAY 168

BELIEVE

Today, don't be overcome by frustration when you encounter a challenge. Just remember, take one step at a time, settle your attitude, and take positive action and execute with all of your energy toward achieving Success! Remember, vocalize that you can do all things through faith and belief. Then commit to that belief!

DAY 169

Today, the ability to innovate is at the heart of creativity. Remember that this is a vital component to any Success. As such, always cultivate an attitude where you are learning and making adjustments along the way. This ability to adjust your process and strategies to best serve your community will allow you to always deal positively with adversity! Always remember that every successful person that ever failed has not ever regarded themselves as a failure!

DAY 170

IMPROVE

Every day in your life presents a new opportunity for you to improve. Always remember to stay committed and use all of your potential to reach your goals! This will give you the momentum needed to face the tough challenges and help you be better than you are today!

DAY 171

Today lift your potential to the highest level; do not begin by focusing on your talent. Instead, begin by harnessing the power of your heart and mind. Remember, your beliefs control everything that you do. So in addition to working smarter rather than harder, it is important that you believe positively, meaning that if you expect to succeed, you will succeed!

DAY 172

CONFIDENCE

Always remember, you can become on the outside what you believe on the inside. So always expect to succeed! This does not always mean that you will, but this level of expectation will always cause you to elevate your talents and keep you moving forward! So today, execute with confidence, and cultivate characteristics that will give you the best opportunities to succeed!

DAY 173

The more you give away, the more you will seem to get to give away! Remember that no matter how much or how little you think you have, you have the ability to do for others what they cannot do for themselves. So today and always, look for these opportunities and seize each moment to make your clients, partners, and all those around you successful!

DAY 174

EXCELLENCE

Always listen to your clients attentively. Ask them what matters, and you will discover what they value. Once you know what matters, offer your very best with no thought of what you would get in return. Remember, always exceed your client's needs and leverage each interaction as an opportunity to overwhelm each person with Excellence and generosity!

DAY 175

Today, take the initiative to recognize opportunities to improve how you serve your community. Remember, you make a living by giving your time, but you make a life by giving your time away!

DAY 176

MOMENTUM

Today and always, allow yourself to dwell in the positive. Remember, sometimes you may get into a rut of negativity and feel that you are not making any progress. If this happens to you, begin again and set achievable goals for yourself. Remember, a pattern of positive achievement will help you develop a pattern of positive momentum, thinking, and results.

DAY 177

Today let the power of hope energize you and provide you with the power to keep on going, even in the tough times. Remember that with hope you can achieve your goals and be successful in everything that you do. So today, as you look toward the future, let the power of hope fuel you with excitement and anticipation!

DAY 178

FAITH

Today, work with the type of determination that destines you for Success! Remember, if you want to succeed, you will have to keep pushing yourself beyond what you think you can do! So today, have faith and finish strong!

DAY 179

Today bring exceptional focus to your work, and whatever the task, seize the opportunity and sweat the small stuff. Remember, hone your abilities, pay close attention to the details, and distill what's best for your clients, partners, and all those that you serve. Remember, focus your energy on what you do well and demonstrate high competence over everything that you do!

DAY 180

POSITIVE ATTITUDE

Today, remember that the way you deal with circumstances reveals many things about your character. So today, if you are faced with adversity, always choose to maintain a hopeful and positive attitude in everything that you do...and you will overcome!

DAY 181

Today and always, follow through with Excellence and exceed expectations in everything that you do! Remember that the qualities of Success demand that you act and perform at the highest levels of Excellence. So today and always be intentional about this principle!

DAY 182

POWER

Today, realize that you hold the power to make all of those that you serve better through the things that you do! Remember, a smile rather than a frown can make someone's day. A kind word instead of criticism may lift any individual's spirit rather than drag them down. So today and always, make a positive impact when interacting with all those around you!

DAY 183

Today and always, maintain a positive attitude in everything that you do. Remember, your attitude gives you a lens on life. So today, take time to reflect on people's expectations, find new ways to do your work, focus on your strengths, and no matter how many times you fall down, pick yourself up and keep on delivering Service Excellence to all those that you serve!

DAY 184

ENTHUSIASM

Today be enthusiastic! Remember, always expect the best and let this be the fuel that allows you to be successful in everything that you do!

DAY 185

Today give it your all! Afford yourself every opportunity to succeed. Remember, even in the trying times, do not quit trying. Rather, show the world the difference in you and stay determined, keep on pressing forward and execute with hard-working persistence!

DAY 186

BELIEVE POSITIVELY

Today and always, think and act out every action as positively as you can! Remember, your life today is a result of your thinking yesterday, and your life tomorrow is essentially determined by what you do and think today!

DAY 187

Today, if it is possible, give those tough situations extra time for creative thinking and effective action planning. Remember, issues may begin to resolve more easily when exposed to the light of time! So today, get energized, reevaluate your priorities, and execute with Excellence and precision!

DAY 188

DRIVE FORWARD

Today take time to appreciate your unique abilities, the resources available to you, your personal history and all of the opportunities around you. Remember, if you objectively identify and discover the desires of your hearts, you will accomplish much and discover a purpose that will help you achieve Success! So today, push yourselves to Act, be an initiator, and remember that whatever gaps you may think you have – your passion will keep you driving forward!

DAY 189

Today, as you confront each situation, execute with hope and positive expectation! Remember, nothing will more quickly and effectively shrivel a bad situation into perspective than focusing your attention on the positive elements of an issue!

DAY 190

COMMITMENT

Today and always, remember that commitment will get you started when others stand still, and it will keep you going when others quit. So stay committed, move toward your goals, and let your heart feel the thrill of pursuing your objectives! Remember, commitment is a key aspect of Success.

DAY 191

Today, forget any challenge or obstacle that stood in the way of your Success, and begin to enlarge your expectations for a bigger and brighter tomorrow. Remember that the Success you achieved yesterday can be achieved again and again!

DAY 192

SERVICE EXCELLENCE

Today and always, do your very best to add value to others. Remember, highly successful people know their purpose, grow to their full potential, and always go above and beyond when serving others!

DAY 193

Today, embrace each positive defining moment. Remember that positive defining moments are a critical part of Success. So today, leverage the Success of those moments when the end result may not have been quite what you may have hoped. Remember that every successful attempt forward eventually leads to being triumphant.

DAY 194

VICTORY

As you prepare for today, take time to reflect on yesterday's victory. Remember, draw on this strength and know that all that was done yesterday will allow you to be successful today!

DAY 195

Today, take positive action, count your blessings, and equip your clients with Excellence! Remember, a successful person will take a frozen situation and heat it up with enthusiasm so they can positively steam forward!

DAY 196

SOLUTION-ORIENTED

Today, use your skills to encourage and deliver above-average solutions to your clients, partners, and all those that you serve! Remember, knowledge is power! But knowledge also empowers! So today, leverage your gifts, skills, and faith as they light the path to Success.

DAY 197

Today, ratchet up your passion! Remember, be dedicated and productive, and increasingly exceed the expectations of your clients. Rekindle your fire and let your heart intensify with all possibilities to achieve Success!

DAY 198

FOCUS

Today, do not ease off when it comes to your work standards. Rather, redouble your efforts and do all things according to the highest standards of Excellence! Remember, be ambitious, focus your energies, and demonstrate enthusiasm as you go the extra mile in serving your clients!

DAY 199

Today, do not limit yourself to past experiences; use each challenge as an opportunity to spring forward and develop your potential. This will help you increase all of your possibilities toward achieving Success! Remember, the future is bright, and when you release yourself and have a limitless attitude, it will open up a pathway for better days ahead!

DAY 200

SUCCESS

Today, use your past experiences to enlarge your expectations for Success!

Remember, experience is sometimes your best teacher, and sometimes, in order for you to experience Success, it could mean you will get tested first and have the benefits of the lessons learned afterwards.

DAY 201

Today, realize that the longer you work, the more you study, and the closer you look, the greater your chances of achieving Success! Remember, see the opportunities when others cannot see anything, and use your skills and abilities to create possibilities that will equip all those that you serve with Excellence!

DAY 202

EXCELLENCE

Today, understand that Success is always
a matter of collaboration and cooperation!
Remember, make your second chances count.
And no matter what has happened in the
past, it's not ever too late to rise above your
past experience, have a bigger purpose, and
go higher than the common plain. So today,
do not compromise, embrace and envision
a brighter beginning, do what is right
and always work with motives that exude
Excellence!

DAY 203

Today, should you encounter challenges or situations that are difficult, remember that you are very capable of rising above the common plain. So stay determined, have faith, embrace hope, and do not quit. Success is always achieved by those who keep on trying!

DAY 204

SUCCESS

Today, remember that the true measure of your Success is not in the position you have reached, but it is in the obstacles you have overcome to reach your desired goals! Remember that Excellence gauges your value by measuring you against your own potential!

DAY 205

Today, stay focused, be committed, and push yourself beyond what you think you can do. Remember, commitment is the one quality above all others that enables you to become successful!

DAY 206

POSITIVE OUTLOOK

Today, embrace a positive outlook and remember, when you feel good about yourself, it will be easier to feel good when you are serving others. Remember that each of us has distinct gifts and enormous potential to achieve Success!

DAY 207

Today, go forward expecting the very best in all things! Remember, a great attitude will give you the fuel to pursue your purpose, grow to your full potential, and help others Succeed! So today, use this principle and you will encounter the staying power to continually improve!

DAY 208

POSITIVE THINKING

Today, look for something positive in everything that you do! Remember that regularly keeping a positive mindset will help you in any type of endeavor. So today, let your actions reflect a high degree of positive thinking!

DAY 209

Today, have an attitude toward the world that reflects Excellence, and in return you will receive excellent results in everything you do. Remember, when you make a decision to have a positive attitude and manage that decision well, there's almost nothing you can't accomplish!

DAY 210

SERVICE EXCELLENCE

Today, give yourself to a cause and create an impact that will be long-lasting. Remember, a successful person will always go a step beyond expectations when filling a need, addressing an issue, and doing what's right when serving others!

DAY 211

Today, one of the best ways to remain positive is to express gratitude and appreciation for everything in life. Remember, when you focus on the positive aspects of each situation, you will move in a positive direction!

DAY 212

SUCCESS

Today and always, seek out teachable moments and strive to learn! Remember, stay hungry, briefly enjoy your Success, always stay calibrated, do not settle or become complacent, and always expect the best outcomes in everything that you do!

DAY 213

Today and always, be a strong achiever, focus on the immediate issue, and then think about the big picture. Remember, embrace your mission and turn every challenging moment into an opportunity to achieve Success!

DAY 214

FINISH STRONG

Today, take time to be supportive, trust one another, and concentrate on the Success of your team!

Remember, see your colleagues through a lens that emanates collaboration and that encourages each person to rise higher, get better and finish strong.

DAY 215

Today, remember, you must have faith and believe that you can succeed if you are going to succeed! Remember, always keep your thought life focused on the good things.

DAY 216

SUCCESS

Today, understand that Success knows its purpose; leveraged correctly, it will fuel you to grow and help others to rise and reach their goals. Remember, when you leverage the energy of exploiting Success, you will be able to surmount the mountain of Service and Excellence!

DAY 217

Today and always, embrace change, think deeply, and work with faith. Remember, master your skills and maintain an attitude that will allow you to have a positive impact on your clients, partners, and everyone you interact with!

DAY 218

EXCELLENCE

Today and always, conduct your business according to the highest standards of Excellence!

Remember to keep these principles in mind:
- Care more than people would expect.
- Expect more than others think would be possible.
- Work smarter and do more than is necessary.

DAY 219

Today and always, maintain a teachable attitude as you approach each situation. Remember, with the right mindset, every challenge becomes an opportunity to succeed!

DAY 220

VALUE

Today, take time to make yourself more valuable, and take steps to expand your knowledge, your experience, and your skills! Remember, as you improve, you will be better able to help others improve!

DAY 221

Today, keep your focus on things that you are able to control. Remember, when you do this each day your tomorrows will get better and better!

DAY 222

SERVICE EXCELLENCE

Today and always, no matter what the circumstance, expect the best and cultivate an attitude that is world-class, that consists of quality and exemplifies Service Excellence. Remember, highly competent people continually search for ways to learn, grow, and improve.

DAY 223

Today, accomplish and deliver more than is expected! Remember, always go the extra mile, do the right things, make principle-based decisions, let action control your attitude, and believe that what you are doing will uncover what others cannot see!

DAY 224

HIGH EXPECTATIONS

Today, go out of your way to do something that will stretch you mentally, emotionally, and physically. Remember, challenges change us for the better. So today, make every new challenge part of your daily walk, and you will always be able to do more than is expected!

DAY 225

Today, leverage your resiliency and tenacity during the toughest assignments. Remember that when challenges arise and results are difficult to achieve, you can be the person who emerges and is looked at to take on the tough jobs. So today, be quick to act and share ideas, and you will naturally find favor from all those around you.

DAY 226

DOING WELL

Today, leave countless marks of doing well for others! Remember, go through your day doing your best to make someone's life good, and remember that a simple smile can make another person's day!

DAY 227

Today, allow yourself to dwell in the positive, and use your most precious commodity (time) to help you commit, prepare, and succeed! Remember, the world has never seen anyone achieve greatness who lacked commitment. So today and always, be committed to Excellence!

DAY 228

SUCCESS

Today, groom yourselves for Success! Remember that Success doesn't suddenly occur; for that matter, neither does failure. Each is a process. So let today prepare you for each moment and let what you do next become the result of what you do today. Remember, we are all living our lives in preparation for something bigger and brighter.

DAY 229

Today, realize that every challenge or problem you face is a blessing in disguise. Remember that each time you encounter something difficult or challenging, it is an opportunity to become stronger, smarter, and more resilient as you voyage through your Success journey!

DAY 230

REFLECT

Today, take time to review your past experiences! Remember, history is a great teacher, and only by taking time to reflect on yesterday can we honestly evaluate its successes and learn how to prepare for tomorrow!

DAY 231

Today, rise above the common plain of living, and commit a little more determination than the average person. Remember, you are better than the average, so take a moment to gain your second wind and develop that potential that has been given to you. Doing this will lift you higher and above the common plain! Remember that Success is achieved and maintained by those who continually keep on trying, pressing forward, and stretching toward Success!

DAY 232

ACHIEVE SUCCESS

The degree of Success you achieve depends upon the amount of sincere desire you possess! Remember that no matter what endeavor you are pursuing, when you throw your heart into your work you will always know Success!

DAY 233

Today become inspired, excited, and determined by seeing the Vision of Success before the prize is won! Remember, victory always begins with Vision.

DAY 234

POSITIVE PERSPECTIVE

Today make it a priority to maintain excellent contact with each person you serve. Remember, connect with others, learn from others, lift each person higher and stay committed to helping each person you interact with cultivate a positive attitude and become mindful of others.

Today, renew your perspective, release your past, and remember your purpose!

DAY 235

Remember, one of the things you must take very seriously is your character, and because of this, your moral compass must always be set for integrity! So today, make sure you are balancing your gifts with your character! Remember, to finish strong, you will need to be humble, convicted, and visionary!

DAY 236

ACHIEVE SUCCESS

An experience is not a failure if it prods you to keep on trying! Remember, there is no failure except in no longer trying. There is no insurmountable barrier until you give up on your purpose. So today, do not limit yourself by your past experiences. Instead, embrace each opportunity and enlarge your expectations. Soon you will increase all of your possibilities to achieve Success!

DAY 237

True generosity begins with the heart! Today, look for ways to serve and add value to others. Remember that greatness is not defined by what a person receives, but by what a person gives! This is a key principle in achieving Success and significance in your life!

DAY 238

EMBRACE HOPE

Today, embrace hope and let its power energize you to keep you going even in the toughest times. Remember that the power of hope will give you the excitement and anticipation of knowing that there is a bright and promising future ahead!

DAY 239

Character, discipline, sacrifice, and tenacity may not be the most fashionable qualities, but they are the surefire ingredients for anyone who wishes to win the race and finish strong. So today, embrace these disciplines and remember, when your Success journey gets challenging, you can count on these qualities to keep you energized and fueled with the power to keep moving forward.

DAY 240

CHARACTER

Today, stay committed, do not cater to convenience, and make all of your decisions based on your rock-steady work ethics. Remember, high-character, disciplined individuals work steadily regardless of the circumstance!

DAY 241

What you do today will define who you can become tomorrow! So remember, having it all does not mean you will have it all at once. Everything takes time, so today, take small steps and concentrate on today. Soon you will find that the slow accumulation of your disciplined action will one day make a big difference!

DAY 242

ACHIEVE EXCELLENCE

Today, work with your end goal in mind! Remember that successful people blaze with desire until their goals come to fruition. So remember, always approach your work with joy and high expectancy! Cease complaining, weed out negativity, and concentrate on opportunities to learn, grow, and achieve Excellence!

DAY 243

Today, work with laser-like focus! Remember, fix your attention on your top priorities, and refuse to be diverted from accomplishing them. Work purposefully, execute with precision, and maximize your energies so that you can give your very best toward everything that you do!

DAY 244

VISION

Today, prioritize your activities so you are able to accomplish what's important and what's next! Remember that your decisions should be based on the purpose of your organization and your overall Vision! So today, let your Vision fuel and power you to fulfill your purpose!

DAY 245

Today, remember that all problems are solvable! The answers may be hidden, but those of you who are willing to be dedicated and stay the course will always find the solution! Remember, when a person tries hard enough and long enough, they will eventually learn, know how much they can accomplish, and find a solution!

DAY 246

COMMITMENT AND EXCELLENCE

Today, reflect on and celebrate the many victories you have won over time! Remember, stay committed to Excellence, guard your thinking, and continue to be confident that your Vision will become a reality!

DAY 247

Today, do not feel discouraged; many setbacks or challenges are the very things that can bring you out on top! Always remember that an opportunity seized is a source for Success. Remember, there is no insurmountable barrier until you give up on your purpose!

DAY 248

SUCCESS

Today, use your past experiences as instruments to mellow your heart, humble your spirit, purify your motives, and increase your sensitivity toward the people you serve as well as those who may be less fortunate! Remember, if you do this well, you will know Success!

DAY 249

Today, do not limit yourself to your past challenges. To do so would be cheating yourself from developing to your fullest potential and increasing all of your possibilities for Success. Rather, begin this week by enlarging your expectations for a brighter tomorrow! Remember that the future is always bright for the pure of heart!

DAY 250

THE FUTURE

Let today's issues be seen as predictors! Remember, the issues or trends you encounter today can help you to prepare and forecast your future!

DAY 251

Today, let yesterday's issues be the answers to today's problems! Remember that each experience is a test, and the benefits of the lessons learned are usually yielded afterwards!

DAY 252

CONFIDENCE

Confidence is a characteristic of a positive attitude! Remember that the greatest achievers have always remained confident regardless of the circumstances. So today, be confident that you will continue to achieve great things!

DAY 253

Today and always, choose to model good character! Remember, your character determines who you are, and who you are and what you do is driven by your lens on life. So today, see the world through a positive lens, and let this reflect and determine the actions you will take!

JEFFREY ABDOOL

DAY 254

EXCELLENCE

Today, follow through with Excellence!
Remember that performing at a high level of
Excellence is always a choice and an act of
will!

DAY 255

Remember, to succeed you must always act with absolute Integrity! So today, add the power of purpose to this characteristic, and you will keep your emotional fire burning!

DAY 256

CHANGE

Today, remain teachable. Try something new, and go out of your way to do something different that will stretch you professionally, mentally, emotionally, or physically! Remember that your growth determines who you are. So let each challenge change you for the better!

DAY 257

Today, remain diligent in doing well, and encourage others to do likewise. Remember that your actions always reflect your degree of discipline!

DAY 258

SUCCESS

Today, keenly focus on your current responsibilities so that you can have a better tomorrow! Remember that your Success journey starts from right where you are, not from where you believe you should be!

DAY 259

Today, be grateful for whatever you have, and courageously do the things you are most afraid to do. Remember that every time you stand up under the weight of adversity, you are being prepared for something great!

DAY 260

LEARNERS' MINDSET

Today, take time to learn something new, and remember that learning is a result of self-discipline and perseverance! So today, maintain a teachable approach and attitude in everything that you do. Remember that successful people are continually embracing a learner's mindset!

DAY 261

Today, enjoy the freedom of empowerment and of making good choices! Remember that when you make a decision, you become a servant to that choice, and you must deal with its consequence, whether it is for better or worse. So remember that successful people make the right decisions early and manage those decisions each day and through the entire Success journey!

DAY 262

FULL POTENTIAL

Today, raise your expectations and seek to go higher than the standards that may be set before you. Remember, great and successful people are not ever satisfied with their current levels of performance! They are demanding on themselves and are continually persisting and pushing hard to reach their fullest potential!

DAY 263

Today, embrace the desire for Success, and master the process of being intentional in everything that you do! Remember, to live on a newer level, you have to think on the highest level!

DAY 264

DISCIPLINED THINKING

Today, surround yourself with thought Leaders and be intentional about having a positive thought life. Remember, find a place where you can shape, stretch, and land your thoughts! Make this a priority and remember, good thinking is a discipline!

DAY 265

Today, remember that when you embrace Wisdom at work and in your life, you wear a lens that affords you the opportunity to act, respond, and execute with calm confidence!

DAY 266

WISDOM

Today, embrace Wisdom and your ability to see life with objectivity! Remember, Wisdom gives you balance, strength, and insight to handle all challenges with rare stability!

DAY 267

One of the secrets to living a life of Excellence is continually maintaining thoughts of Excellence! Remember, living differently begins by thinking differently!

DAY 268

CHOICES

The thoughts in your mind will always be more important than the things in your life! Remember, you cannot buy or win happiness. You must choose it!

DAY 269

Today, find something positive in everything that you do! Remember, work hard, work joyfully, work purposefully, and be determined to turn yesterday's challenges and difficulties into today's breakthrough moments!

DAY 270

BLESSINGS

Today, find at least one opportunity to share with someone how grateful you are for whatever you have accomplished. Remember, every day you have an opportunity to express gratitude and appreciation for life's blessings!

DAY 271

Today, embrace good thinking and let this
be your foundation toward achieving great
results. Remember that to make progress in
any area will require action! And the Success
of that action will depend greatly on your
thinking beforehand!

DAY 272

WINNING

Today, bring a spirit of collaboration and cooperation into everything you do! Remember, think Win-Win-Win, meaning, as you collaborate with others, you win, they win, and the team wins!

DAY 273

Today, embrace joy, peace, patience, kindness, goodness, faithfulness, gentleness, and self-control in everything that you do! Remember that life is like a mirror: what you show is what you see; what you put in is what you get out!

DAY 274

EXCELLENCE

Today, focus on achieving positive results, and allow your good works to contribute to the Success and betterment of others. Remember, commit yourself to Excellence, and you will enjoy a productive lifestyle!

DAY 275

Today, focus your actions on delivering a positive experience to your clients, associates, and everyone you may come into contact with. Remember that Success is not accident, luck, or fate! It is the realization of persistence and a progressive sense of predetermined action!

DAY 276

POSITIVE PRINCIPLE

Today, extract every positive principle that you can from your experiences and your life. Remember, constantly be on the lookout for anything that will help you enhance and improve your chances of achieving your goals!

DAY 277

Today, let what you see be determined by your perspective on life as well as your level of discernment, and let what you seek be based on your values and purpose. Remember, you can respond to an issue based on what you see as well as what you seek!

DAY 278

PURPOSE

Today, work with a strong sense of purpose, and let that be the difference between the ordinary and the extraordinary action you will take! Remember that a person who works with purpose will always do things out of the ordinary and above average!

DAY 279

Today, choose the best course of action and move forward! Do not stop once you start! Look at the issue, choose your best course of action, and relentlessly go after it! Remember that every issue is solvable!

DAY 280

POSITIVE ATTITUDE

Today, should adversity arise, embrace it with a positive attitude. This will give you the fuel required to pursue your purpose and provide you the staying power needed to continually improve! Remember that the greatest determinant of tomorrow's Success is today's Success. So go into each day expecting the best!

DAY 281

Today make it priority to maintain Excellent contact with each person you serve. Remember, go out of your way to connect with others, learn from every experience, do your best to lift each person higher and always stay committed to helping everyone you interact with cultivate a positive attitude as well as being exceedingly others-minded.

DAY 282

DISCIPLINED THINKING

Today, embrace the will to do what's right! Remember that disciplined thinking is doing what you really don't want to do so that you can do what you really want to do! Keep this in mind, and regularly take on challenges that will develop the kind of disciplined thinking that will help you with whatever you endeavor to do!

DAY 283

Today, practice the power of Integrity. Be consistent with how you act and how you treat everyone, always honor all, and act ethically at all times. Remember, to climb the mountain of Success, you will need the power of Integrity to propel you upward and forward!

DAY 284

TRUTH

Today, do what is right regardless of whether anyone is looking! Remember, there is something very powerful in doing what is good, right, and true!

DAY 285

Today, be disciplined to do the right thing. Remember, you are an ordinary person with an extraordinary amount of determination. So today, let your character be defined as the sum of your behaviors, both public and private, and consistently enact these disciplines across the spectrum of your life for all to see!

DAY 286

VISION MINDED

Today, allow your commitment to free you to do great things! Remember, the greatest days of our lives are the days when we sense our commitment is at the highest degree. So today and always, be mission- and vision-minded!

DAY 287

Today, prioritize your time and focus your energies on the tasks that will give you the highest returns! Remember, Excellence comes from doing the right things right! So today, evaluate your priorities, plan your time carefully, and follow through on the things that matter most!

DAY 288

POSITIVE ATTITUDE

Today, think about your unique abilities, the resources available to you, and all of the opportunities around you. Remember that the happiest people in life simply make the best out of every situation and are in constant agreement that everything will go well!

DAY 289

When you think about your Success journey, remember that Success is continual, it is an ongoing process, and most of all, it is the positive result of steady forward movement! So today, be intentional about everything that you do, and work with the purpose of making every action count! Remember, focus on doing the right things right and then following through in a consistent way!

DAY 290

SUCCESS

Today, do everything you can to serve your community well. Concentrate on this goal and focus your potential on continually exceeding your clients' expectations. Then you will reach your full potential and experience Success beyond your imagination. Remember, the true measure of Success can be measured between what you might have been and what you will become. In other words, Success comes as a result of growing to your fullest potential.

DAY 291

Remember, at one point or another, you will come to a place where capacity and capability are stretched beyond your abilities and gifts. So today, let these instances become a catalyst that drives you toward Success!

DAY 292

GIVING

Today, embrace your relationships with your families, friends, business partners, and clients! Remember that the greatest thing you need to achieve Success resides in your abilities to connect, appreciate, trust, and be in harmony with all those that you interact with. So today, dedicate yourselves to thinking it forward and having an attitude where you are increasingly giving, serving, and investing in the Success of others. Remember, the highest level of living always comes from giving!

DAY 293

Today and always make sure you do your homework. Remember, that your defense against a negative situation will change when you define the issue, gather information from credible sources, brainstorm on options, seek advice from the right people, listen to your instincts, and make decisions based on the principles and values you believe in. So today, be Successful in all that you do, and make sure you do your homework.

DAY 294

PERSEVERANCE

Today, if your heart's desire is focused on achieving Success, you will have to have courage, strength, and resilience! Remember that no matter how difficult or challenging a circumstance may be, you can always find a way to persevere.

DAY 295

Every stage of life presents lessons to be
learned. We can choose to be teachable
and continue to learn, or we can be closed-
minded; the decision is yours. So today and
always, seek out teachable moments and strive
to learn! Remember, with every learning
experience, always expect the best outcome!

DAY 296

FORWARD LOOKING

Today and always, keep trying, move forward, and overcome every challenge or obstacle with absolute persistence! Remember, for every goal and strategy you have, one of the most important ingredients for Success is persistence!

DAY 297

Today, forget any challenge or obstacle that stood in the way of Success, and begin to enlarge your expectations for a bigger and brighter tomorrow! Remember that when you limit yourself to your past experiences, you may cheat yourself from developing your potential and increasing the many possibilities to achieving Success.

DAY 298

ENDURANCE

Today, when you encounter challenging situations, do not let those situations deter you from meeting and exceeding your goals. Endure, Improve, and Overcome! Remember that trying times are not the time to quit trying, so work with determination and push well beyond what you think you can do! You are capable of much more than you think!

DAY 299

Today leverage the power of breakthrough moments. Remember, to release the power of a breakthrough moment; you will need the full strength of your team, you will need to be glad to share the spotlight with everyone and most importantly, you will need be like an open book and be fully transparent.

Remember, the winning teams have winning team members and are filled with breakthrough people. So today and always, be confident that you are always just one breakthrough moment away from achieving Success over any situation!

DAY 300

POSITIVE ATTITUDE

Today, rely on your positive attitude to get you through the day! Remember:

- Expect the best in everything that you do.
- Always remain upbeat.
- See solutions in every problem or issue.
- Always believe in yourself.
- If you have stumbled, always hold on to hope!

No matter what happens, embrace a positive attitude, and it will help get you through all circumstances!

DAY 301

Today, as you go through your day, expect the best of everything; expect the best treatment from your service partners, expect the best interactions with your clients, and expect that you will succeed in everything that you do! Remember that your attitude has a profound influence over the outcome of everything you do!

DAY 302

POSITIVE ACTION

Today be intentional, make every action count, make the right choices, empower your clients, and maximize all of your talents by living your life to your fullest potential! Remember that life is a matter of choices, and each of us has the power to make the right choices!

DAY 303

Today, always let your values guide you! Remember, your core values must be held deeply and must authentically describe who you are, and just like circumstances, the way you live your life is constantly changing. You acquire new skills, disciplines, and practices and sometimes your practices may even change. However, the one thing that must always remain constant is your core values!

DAY 304

SELF-DISCIPLINE

Today, master your emotions! Do not let your feelings prevent you from doing what you should or drive you to do things that you shouldn't! Remember, self-discipline dictates how effectively you use your time, and disciplined and successful people will always maximize their time! So today, keep your mind active, and regularly take on mental challenges to develop the kind of disciplined thinking that will help you with whatever endeavor you need to do!

DAY 305

Success is a state of mind! So today, win the war over your thinking and let your positive attitude transform every challenge into an opportunity! Remember that the better your attitude, the more likely you will be able to overcome any challenge, grow, learn, and, most of all, move forward on your Success journey!

DAY 306

SUCCESS

Today have faith that all things will work out as they should! Remember that Success is always attainable when it is defined correctly and when we make the effort to do the best that we are capable of doing!

DAY 307

Remember that the path to Success lies in the realization that there is always room to learn and improve! So today, take meaningful steps toward developing, learning from each situation, and creating pivotal defining moments that make a positive impact on each interaction with another person! Remember, to teach is to learn!

DAY 308

COLLABORATION

Victories can only be secured when you work together! Today you can reshuffle your plans and work with the anticipation of Success! Remember that with every delay you have more time to plan, learn, and gain valuable feedback that will allow you to capitalize on each experience!

DAY 309

Today, you can achieve much Success in this world! Remember, when you find a need, fill it; when you face a challenge, meet it head on; when you develop your plans, execute with the utmost precision; and when you are developing your talents and skills, share your knowledge with all those that you serve!

DAY 310

PATIENCE

Opportunities will always come more than once if you are patient! So today, remember, there will be another chance if you're looking, knocking, and willing to travel another path to reach your goals!

DAY 311

Remember that each challenge you encounter will leave you a little better after it is resolved and gone. So today, stay committed to the successful fulfillment of your stated mission and begin your task knowing you will finish with Excellence!

DAY 312

JOY AND EXPECTANCY

Today work with sustained Excellence! Blaze a trail with desire and see your Vision come to fruition. Remember, execute with the end in mind, and approach your work with joy and high expectancy!

DAY 313

Today get ignited and no longer shrink when barriers are in front you! Rather, conceive all possibilities and opportunities to progress forward and drive Service Excellence! Remember, passion will give you the momentum to succeed in everything that you do, and it will ensure you keep your edge over the competition! So today, let your passion make the impossible possible!

DAY 314

PRIORITIES

Today, work with laser-like focus. Fix your attention on your highest priorities and refuse to be diverted from accomplishing your goals! Remember, work purposefully and strategically, and always do what is important rather than what is easy.

DAY 315

Today, see yourselves through a positive lens!
Remember that the better you picture yourself,
the greater your performance and abilities to
develop to your fullest potential!

DAY 316

OPPORTUNITIES

Today, cease to complain, and weed
out negative thoughts from your mind!
Remember, always monitor your attitude, and
concentrate on opportunities that will allow
you to learn, grow, and succeed!

DAY 317

Today, adjust your thinking, and change your patterns of action. When a pivotal moment alerts you to the possibility of acting, bring about positive change, and adjust your approach so that each experience becomes a lasting breakthrough. Remember, breakthrough moments happen when you seize an opportunity that has been presented by a significant event. So today, be intentional about everything you do, make every action count, make the right choices, empower your clients, and maximize all of your talents by living your life to your fullest potential. Remember that life is a matter of choices, and each of us has the power to make the right choices!

DAY 318

ACHIEVING SUCCESS

Today and always, surround yourself with smart, passionate, motivated people who think differently from you! Look for the value in their ideas and seek different perspectives. Remember that this is one of the key drivers of intelligence gathering and is certainly a key driver behind achieving Success!

DAY 319

Today, remember that Integrity is a result of self-discipline, inner trust, and the decision to be relentlessly honest in all situations. Integrity is the glue that holds our way of life together. So today, constantly strive to keep your Integrity intact, and allow your Integrity to be the personal referee in all of your decision-making processes!

DAY 320

OPPORTUNITIES

Today give it your all! Afford yourself every opportunity to succeed. Remember that the difference maker in all that you do is always based on staying determined and working with hard persistence!

DAY 321

Today, do not dwell on what's wrong with a given situation. Rather, coach yourself and eliminate the negative self-talk you may hear. Remember, there are possibilities in every situation! So see the positive potential despite the circumstances, look for the good, look for how to improve, strive for Excellence, keep the right attitude, seek out your inner strength, cultivate it, and find the positive possibility in every situation!

DAY 322

SUCCESS

Today, think about a recent setback, and then determine that no matter how difficult the circumstance, you will remain committed to overcome. Remember that every achiever takes responsibility to its highest level, learns from each situation, and realizes that from the very moment they hit a setback, it's time to ratchet up their commitment and do whatever it takes to achieve and attain Success!

DAY 323

Today, no matter how tough it gets or what kind of storm comes, use these moments as opportunities to learn, grow, improve, serve, and distinguish yourself as a possibility thinker! Remember, if you believe you can, you can! So be intentional about everything that you do! Learn from each challenge and maintain a mindset where you live and learn! Continually do this, and you will learn how to live at the highest level!

DAY 324

POSITIVE ATTITUDE

If at first you do not succeed, try something harder! This means that to get to the next level, you need to push the envelope, take more chances, expand your thresholds, and increase your opportunities to achieve Success! Remember that you cannot walk the second mile until you have walked the first! So today, maintain a positive, hopeful attitude, and believe that with each step forward you are getting better and better!

DAY 325

Today, seize the day and make every action count! Remember, to improve the world around us, you must focus your attention on helping and serving others!

DAY 326

INTEGRITY

Everything you do flows from the person you are! Today, be yourself, be the best person you can be, and as you serve, grow, and learn, focus your actions and communications in a way that creates a positive impact on others! Remember, when you live a life that is based on Integrity, it will always promote trust, Success, and the highest level of living!

DAY 327

Today, realize the value of taking small steps
toward your goal. Remember, always think
big and start small! So today, if you are going
to win, you will need to begin by leveraging
each incremental accomplishment and letting
that provide you with energy, motivation,
and encouragement toward accomplishing
the next steps out in front of you. Remember,
small beginnings afford you the opportunity
to prioritize, concentrate, and succeed!

DAY 328

CONFIDENCE

Today, concentrate your thinking on your potential and every possibility of achieving Success! Remember that the more confidence and skills you build, the greater your chance of overcoming each challenge!

DAY 329

Today, pay attention to your intuition and follow through with Excellence! Remember, always stay committed, make principle-based decisions, let your action control your attitude, and believe it, then see it!

DAY 330

GIVING

Today, go out of your way to be helpful, supportive, courteous, polite, and considerate to every individual you may come into contact with! Remember, give until it feels good, and always embrace these timeless traits!

DAY 331

Happiness is in many things. It's in caring, helping, sharing, giving, etc. Today, let your happiness manifest in being at peace with yourself and knowing that you are making an effort, a full effort, to do your very best!

Remember, the greatest joy in life comes from doing something for someone else without any thought of getting something in return!

DAY 332

PATIENCE

Today embrace the art of patience! Remember, good and worthwhile things always take time!

DAY 333

Today, have an excellent outlook on everything you do, be a no-limits thinker, be unwilling to accept the accepted, walk the edge of each issue, and be very determined to maximize your efforts to exploit your fullest potential each day. Remember that this type of positive perspective will give you an edge in everything that you do!

DAY 334

IMPROVE

Today concentrate on continually improving! Remember, sharpen your mind, control your emotions, and focus your actions so that each day you become a little better than you were yesterday!

DAY 335

Today, should you encounter a challenging situation that may seem difficult, remember that you are very capable of rising above the common plain and achieving Success. So today, stay determined, have faith, embrace hope, and do not quit. Success is always achieved by those who keep on persisting and pressing forward!

DAY 336

SUCCESS

Today work with joy and expectancy! Remember that when you work with your whole heart and a sustained perspective of Excellence, your desire to attain Success will come to fruition!

DAY 337

Today, if you are confronted by the weight of any adversity, you can endure, improve, and overcome! In fact, you can use these moments as momentum builders and create the type of forward progress that turns every challenge into a possibility. Remember that passion is the prerequisite for Success and high achievement!

DAY 338

POSITIVE MOTIVES

Today, keep your motives right, build positive relationships, and be inclined to put others ahead of your own agenda! Remember that when you do things for the right reasons, it gives you the inner strength to spring forward when things may not go as expected!

DAY 339

Nearly all successes are the fruit of taking initiative! Today, when you enter into the arena of action, be strategic, take responsibility, take time to assess your priorities, and focus your energies on the things that are really important and that matter! Remember that when you focus your passion on what's most important, your skill set climbs to new heights, and you continually advance in the direction of Success!

DAY 340

INTEGRITY

Always perform your work to the highest level
of your ability! Today, focus your thinking,
harness your energy, keep your word, walk
your talk, and model alignment between
beliefs, words, and actions. Remember,
determine which decisions are most important
and dedicate scheduled time toward
addressing them!

DAY 341

Today, embrace the joy of creative thinking!
Remember that creativity is being able to see
what no one else has seen and thinking what
nobody else has thought so that you can do
what no one else has done! So today, let's
break some new ground, move along the lines
of innovation, and help others do old things in
new ways!

DAY 342

STRATEGIC THINKING

Today, release the power of Strategic Thinking! Remember, thinking strategically means you are planning, becoming more efficient, maximizing your strengths, and finding the most direct path to achieving your goals!

DAY 343

Today, be precise about your thinking and intentional about how you engage each issue or task. Remember that when you are strategic about your approach, you build the type of credibility that will continually increase your potential for Success tomorrow!

DAY 344

BELIEVE

Today, embrace the energy of possibility type thinking! Remember that when you believe you can do something that is difficult and you succeed, many possibilities open for you! So today, accomplish those tasks that seem impossible because when you believe in the solutions you are driving, miraculous things will happen!

DAY 345

Today, choose to face every challenge with Courage! Remember, like many character qualities, Courage comes from within, and it begins with the decision to make a choice and follow through! So today, while others wait to see what's going to happen, step forward, rise above the common plain, and meet each challenge knowing that you will achieve and experience the very best outcomes!

DAY 346

EXPECTANCY

Go into this day with a high level of expectancy! Remember that successful people will expect the best and operate with a created belief that what they do is so powerful, that somehow or someway they will always achieve their goals and make things happen! So today, dwell in the positive moments and give your best in every situation!

DAY 347

Today, stand firm and come to the realization that in the face of adversity you will persevere. Remember, always have a positive mindset, and cultivate an attitude and approach where you are allowing your strengths to fuel you with the energy required to achieve small wins and long term victory over each situation. Do this well, and no matter the circumstance, you will know Success!

JEFFREY ABDOOL

DAY 348

POSITIVE ACTION

Today, manage your energy well! Remember that your energy drives your ability to perform consistently well! So go into the week fulfilling your objectives, exceeding expectations, and filling your time with experiences that will help you keep your energy level high. Remember, to elevate your energy to the highest level, it is important that each action you take encourages and adds value to others! Do this well, and your energy levels will soar!

DAY 349

Remember that enthusiasm flows naturally when you are acting and doing things with passion! This limitless energy can help you achieve your goals! So today, leverage your passion, and do your very best to add value, expand your knowledge, and improve the quality of your service to others!

DAY 350

EXCELLENCE

Today, be an encourager and take a servant's action to bring about a positive outcome in everything that you do! Remember, embrace this mindset, and you will soar to the highest levels of Excellence!

DAY 351

The next time you're touched by a significant issue or event, look for ways to adjust your thinking and behavior so that instead of temporary enlightenment, you experience lasting breakthrough! Remember, we are developing and learning daily! So today, embrace each positive defining moment and allow these experiences to ignite your passion so that they make the impossible possible!

DAY 352

PASSION

Today, allow your passion to enable you to plow through, jump across, or dig under any obstacle. Remember, when others see a dead end, let your passion see possibilities. Remember that passion sees no unstoppable barriers!

DAY 353

Today, do your very best with your time; demonstrate the best of who you are through your character, Integrity, actions, and abilities! Identify what is most important and get those things done! Remember, make the right decisions early and manage these decisions each and every day!

DAY 354

POSITIVE OUTLOOK

Today, start your day knowing and declaring that it is going to be a great day! Remember that your attitude at the beginning of any situation can affect its outcome more than anything else! So let all that is well begin well!

DAY 355

Today, focus and concentrate on achieving Success! Remember, set your priorities in a manner that will make the best use of your time because your time is precious and valuable, and while you cannot change time, you can change and control your priorities!

DAY 356

BREAKTHROUGH MOMENTS

Great thinking precedes great results! So today, think big picture! Remember, think beyond yourself, take a holistic approach, gain clarity over each issue, and think outside of the box so that you can explore ideas and options that will allow you to experience breakthrough moments!

DAY 357

Today, unleash the power of possibility type thinking! Remember, when you look at each situation through the lens of possibilities, it means that you are using your enthusiasm and hope to find solutions for even the seemingly impossible situations!

DAY 358

FOCUS

Today focus on the positive! Remember, an issue solved is a springboard for future Success! The key is to focus on what you are learning, as well as to concentrate on what you are doing. So today, listen to others, listen with your heart, and remain humble, and you will begin to learn and see things that will help you resolve issues and succeed! Remember, focus on these things each day, and it will positively impact all you do!

DAY 359

Remember that your commitment is tested every day! So today, if things get hectic, life gets rough, or the challenges become too great, remember to stay determined, stay committed, and embrace the qualities of your tenacity to accomplish the things that are most important! Do these things daily, and make the decision to commit wholeheartedly to everything that you do!

DAY 360

EXCELLENCE

Today, redouble your efforts to do things according to the highest standards of Excellence. Focus yourself professionally, pursue your goals, and always sow seeds that will benefit others. Go into your day with an attitude like it's going to be your best day! Remember that successful people have a strong habit of believing that the best things will happen!

DAY 361

Today, refuse to give into excuses, work hard, stay determined, keep a service mind set, and be committed to strive for Excellence! Remember, Excellence means doing your very best in everything, in every way, every single day!

DAY 362

CHOICE

Today, choose to grow beyond your natural talent. Choose to make good choices. Choose not to blame your circumstances. Choose to be responsible for the person you are becoming. Remember, bring a high standard to everything that you do and make Excellence your standard!

DAY 363

Today embrace each challenge! Remember that each challenge in front of you is an opportunity for a creative, alternative solution!

DAY 364

POSITIVE IMPACT

Today, pause for a moment to gain clarity over each situation, embrace truth, and plan to carry out everything that you do with Excellence! Remember that the one thing that can help guarantee Success when faced with a difficult or challenging situation, is to have faith from the beginning that you can achieve your goals!

DAY 365

Today, take action to do something that will make a positive impact on someone's life (client, associate, friend, family, or anyone). Remember that nothing improves a person's outlook more than providing or delivering a service to someone with a greater need than their own! Remember, the highest level of Success is reached by helping those in need!

TODAY & ALWAYS

Today, believe in what you say, then live what you say. Remember, there is no greater credibility than conviction in Action! So today, always remember the goal that everything you put your mind to must be Actionable!

Every day of our lives is a preparation for the next and what you become tomorrow is a direct result of each action you take today. So today, groom yourselves for Success and remember, the way you live today prepares you for tomorrow.

Today, lift your talents to the highest level and do not begin by focusing on your talent. Instead begin by harnessing the power of your heart and mind. Remember, your beliefs control everything that you do. So in addition to working smarter rather than harder, it is important that you believe positively! Meaning that if you expect to succeed, you will succeed!

I have always believed that we all have the power to positively impact the outcome of any situation we may encounter. Today, start your day by knowing and declaring that it is going to be a great day. Remember, our attitudes at the beginning of any situation can affect its outcome more than anything else. So today, let all that is well begin well!

You are blessed with unique gifts, skills, and the type of faith which lights a path to achieve Success. So today, use your skills to encourage and deliver above-average solutions to your Clients, partners and all those that you serve. Remember, Knowledge is power. But Knowledge also Empowers!

Today, adjust your thinking and change your patterns of action and when a pivotal moment alerts you to the possibility of acting, bring about positive change and adjust your approach so that each experience becomes a lasting breakthrough.

Remember, breakthrough moments happen when you seize an opportunity that has been presented by a significant event. So today, be intentional about everything you do, make every action count, make the right choices, empower your Clients and maximize all of your talents by living your life to the fullest potential. Remember, life is a matter of choices and each of us has the power to the make the right choices!

Today's circumstances can reveal key things about our character. Remember, if you are faced with adversity you can choose two paths: character or compromise. So today and always, choose character and maintain a hopeful and positive attitude in everything that you do!

368

ABOUT THE AUTHOR

Jeff Abdool is Senior Executive Leader with over thirty years of business and technical experience with one of America's Fortune 100 organizations. At the age of sixteen, he started his Success journey and for the past thirty years, he has had an unparalleled commitment to a single organization. His deepest business values are rooted with integrity, trust, kindness, Excellence, joy, peace, patience, goodness, faithfulness, gentleness, self-control, and Servant Leadership. His entrepreneurial nature comes through in this book and he is sure you will be motivated and blessed with each Positive Thought for the Day!

40863201R00211

Made in the USA
Middletown, DE
25 February 2017